Birds
of the
West

Birds
of the
West

David Bromige

The Coach House Press   1973

ACKNOWLEDGMENTS

Some of these poems were first made public through the agency of the editors of the following magazines & books: *Buttons, Caterpillar, Hudson Review, Imago, Open Reading, Paper Pudding, Poetry Review, Spectrum, The Fact So Of Itself.*

Printed in Canada

The Coach House Press
401 Huron Street (rear)
Toronto, Ontario M5S 2G5

Cover by David Hlynsky

For Sherril
& Chris
& Sterling
& Markus
& Dylan
& Karen
& Ann, & all
who happily
make up
the company
of the hill,
not in this order
necessarily
but what it means,
one by one by one

Birds of the West

"If a bird happens to come into the room
I'm in, I get terrified & leave. The
poor bird has to fend for itself as best
it can. I might just possibly open the
window."

—Ingmar Bergman

A Rime

The great horned owl —
I call you, never having seen you
to my satisfaction, though that flapping
darker than the eucalyptus branches
the night I did go looking —

but the hoo-hoo-hu-hoo, that's the sign
my book identifies you by. Believed to presage
death, it says. And that that's incorrect,
but not entirely, you hoot to scare up game
— or hoot, & scare up game —

some animal that, safe,
takes alarm, scurries out,
as if to meet you —

you call at intervals
so spaced I think them regular,
count, & it comes again, I come
to count on it. One morning

a large owl perching on our boundary-fence
couldn't't'v been you, the book says
likely the short-eared kind,
it often flies by day. I was eating breakfast,

suddenly, an unexpected presence — I looked up
or felt what I had glimpsed, & then
looked out — at such a matter-of-factness.
That then flew off. I shook, with what it was.

Your call comforts, I prefer it to the silence,
now I think of that, that most nights are.
I — said with much assurance,

a place to be
even as this well-lit house,
beside the fire. Say I was tired,
cold, & somewhere out in it —

if you didn't call I can imagine
calling for you,
if only to enter the trance.

Next love

The heat put it in my mind
I guess, so when I saw that glow
on the horizon eastward, growing
while I watched, the prairie
all around me dry, ready for fire

my excitement told me
this was what I saw, burning
everywhere, fixed
by the wonder for five minutes
when I thought about it later, when I thought
to run back to the house & let them know

there was something someone ought to cope with,
somehow. Before I could the flickering
I'd read out of the wavering
as flame, congealed

till what was then revealed
as a huge moon, began its rise
to be a second marvel, a moon that large & orange,
complete,
          contained —

then the familiar
diminishment & paling as it rode
higher, that ache
asking some participation that its shape
refuses, a lonely
circle, where the poem begins.

*North Battleford Saskatchewan, August 1949 —
Sebastopol California July 1971.*

"Dear Night"

Dear night — that permits
my face to be reflected in
this window, yet
creates the village lights behind,
beyond,
            let me repeat
that story which you tell,

I am alone here,
the woman I live with has driven to the city,
my limbs face body are
still firm & I desire them

while of all these constellations
Bloomfield's 7 street lights only
shimmer as if a car, the unlikely
old girlfriend at the wheel, might
even now draw near

night, you are since I perceive you
& I exist in that perception &
praise you as you verify my being.
Let the less fortunate
fret out their fates. Night,

figure of speech, this voice
within my lovely head
says,
        As if a landslide had
buried me entirely

the world proceeds, Bloomfield even
can't see me,
                she comes,

blesses with her quick
vivaciousness

nothing, she is not here.
Remember
night in the tale how I
dug this self free to
find the lover, naked we
made it then paraded through that
cheering crowd, each & every eye
upon me till I glimpsed
you, whispering
Blind, all blind — incredulous
I noticed how within the undeniable
look of life each bright
organ sustained a piece of you at center
where surely you must know
that what you say is true —

thus I have no more shame before you
than if I'd driven down to town to pass
time drinking or
listening among a throng to songs
asserting multiply our presences

& let her take me in your sight
& thus our night of loving is
spent, muttering one to the other
of aloneness, as if
naming a lost lover.

So that/the opaque world

The body's there so that the legs
may be attached & they
in turn are necessary
to get the body *to* someplace
where food can turn to energy
to keep the body whole & power the legs.

A spider just went by
but this above's my parents' calvinism,
a vestigial Idea
lurking in their actions
as I was growing up,

& moving as all such
to eat, in order that,
etcetera. While I
sat in a chair & 'idly' read
until something should catch the eye
set in my head, a spider
just went by but
oh-oh, he
she or it is
headed back again! Fly
to the typewriter to discover
what it has in mind,

a human universe is made of this, a universe
endures the making's terms,
we make that evident. When I am tired
spiders such as this
drop to the bed & something
bites me, when I sleep

ırcease of hunger
ls me, but the dreams
ıger like long meals,
ım that stuff & bite my nails
vake, but typing
events that,
state of readiness

ınting to admit
me understanding,
m afraid my life will waste —

any act, even if it be to 'turn my back'
pears a form thereof,
ough spoken through the opaque world,
my delight.

"This time not shot"

This time not shot —
unmarked by any accident,
no sheen yet of decay —
no blurring of your form —

this much one knows,
a disease of life
has done for you. Maybe
it's how lifelike you looked,

dull brown & yellow,
makes me tremble,
now as then — the day
I found you,

making you seem vulnerable.
Then as now the thin
thing poking like a frozen flickering
out from the opened beak

most catches me.
I must'v heard you sing.
Dad tells me
mother loved the birds. A fact

I remembered when he said.
She died
far away from me
in time as space.

Nor is there any link
between the two
excepting where I think
in the circuits of this brain.

You do not come again
or words are ghosts.
But then you are not here
for all I would present

went with the time —
but some idea
with you within
presses out these words.

This is some other form —
nothing is saved in it
from all our distances
but distance,

distance, distance singing,
to be kept
from us, & the shining
that the mind

imposes, on what
if not the mind
insists is different —
your death & life

suffering no interference
if this form to hold
my grief is risen
from these thoughts concerning you —

acknowledging you've gone beyond
what any one can remedy,
experiencing the chance of waste,
in this perplexity

about identity,
between the dead & living,

where she is always present,
whose breasts & arms were

where language thought & feeling all
began in me, because
these three are one
& make me want to see a frozen tongue.

Person

I want to lie in the earth
with a rifle & pick off
strangers that pass in cars.
Who knows me, really.
It's all an act. But secretly
someone is alive in here,
someone I want you to meet.

CLOSE

Somewhere they lie —
close, that couple
who compel
any one among us
& our compromises

with them, 2
& 3, 4's & 5's, &
6's — I
recently got married
— to race ahead,

that's their urging,
but when did you
first find yourself
aware of them,
I was eleven,

saw them in my mind,
in my mind's eye,
reached down a hand
quickened by my tongue
as if to touch them,

evoking, even to command
their presence, how often since
to be commanded in my turn —
the entrances were fearsome then,
hard to be believed, & torment

could attend on
each attempt. Today
they're easily encountered,

a courtesan possesses
an infinitude of dresses

inflaming with such various
guises, to always the same pitch —
the woman in the restaurant,
the woman on the plane,
the one who met the plane,

wanting to be singularly
real, to the stranger each was
next to, or hoping I
might be the next
to bring us to the same.

What is it? Cattle
stretching through a fence —
"glands" — the "threat &
promise of dissolving to sheer
energy" — how the legs feel,

after, as though floating —
but something further,
look at the profusion
everywhere, of forms with faces
fronting them, not ours,

yet similar, however
absolutely other —
hear the pleas, I am
going to split, there
is nothing here, for me —

I wanted to be famous,
wanted to discover

where that lever was,
to shift the whole,
wanted to be loved,

by one, by everyone —
how they couple,
while I sit here writing
Now they couple, writhing,
the woman I am living with

is sleeping, but
this afternoon we were
visiting their couch —
but then I woke —
to the distances of hills

about this house, a radio
crackling with static,
an incoherent friend —
morsels of so-called news,
important

beyond my understanding
of what each means to me —
to wonder any longer they are
so adored, with impenetrable ease
accessible —

see the legs like fingers forked —
but I would talk to you
being human, of them, though you hear
as I do, as they do,
how they are asleep.

Outside

The fog so thick
that when I stepped outside
just now, the house-lights
threw my shadow, huge, against it —
I guess the Specter of the Brocken
much the same.
                    Condensing on the trees
it falls like rain,
the barren clay,
where I took such strolls last summer,
is thick these days, with grass.
What solitude

& silence, outside there — in quality
different from being in a forest, this is mainly
open range, but the solitude is common
to my thought. I thought

characters with mighty limbs,
furred, as cave-bears yes,
but more immediately
furred as trees with moss —

having believed — say, felt the force —
those tales of Bigfoot have,
among the redwoods, all alone
yet not, animals, perhaps inimical,
brush, furred, against the vegetable
forms life also takes —

an intermediary
partaking of our, human, traits
yet of the horror also

that the forest holds, as one
faces him self in to it,

has its necessity — huge
as trees are huge, that threaten us,
if such be felt. Some tales
will show them friendly,
human children play with them,
they could, I know,
defend me. A certain logic maybe

favors them, says this voice
I place within my head,
& logic,
            condensed
in my imagination.

For Tom Thumb, A Relation & A Measure

I might'v taken you for a magic prince
with a finger into everything, nowhere
I looked but, once I'd learned of you,
you pranced, or crept — inched along,
they'd said — no place but bore, not
like a snail's, not utterly, your print

for all it was invisible, the cloak
giving you that power that even now
tenses my hand because my eyes think
how you are, no bigger than the top
joint of my thumb —

hadn't you, as I, been huge, once. For now
you were my hero because I was too small,
because you too, although, like me, you
couldn't help it, often didn't fit. I
tired, I mostly went away, with this one of
them, or that — whoever was dealing with the child

I sided with. For they were right
as they were big, as things
proved difficult, as they knew
how to shift them, or give up.

I gave up you. I named you anything,
& if it grew, then you
were multiplied, you had no soul
& thus served anywhere. A key
depressed again & again on the piano
as traffic noises rose, or wind
shook in the grasses,
in the ears.
                    A life, a phrase of theirs, went on,

some days as fixed
as notches on a stick,
some days as arbitrary. There was nothing
you corresponded with
but those exactly like yourself,

rendering your trip unnecessary.
Did a feeling
stir, a casual look
did to show the way it went,

with them, I was safe, together we were
huge, commanding everything. I heard
you were an island, off the coast of Scotland,
some archaic exile,
stalking the moors, the cliffs,
too real for company & trumpeting

the secret names of friends, of children
to the wind that ruffles,
as from the literal peat the smoke
hangs motionless, straight up,
the pages of a dictionary.

When you were one among a dozen
& I reached in among that litter
to hold you on my little finger
weighing just an ounce
I swore a fealty

yet that was to reality,
if I betrayed you since
hadn't you brought that on yourself,
another of their fancies merely —

then how do you return,
what term of spell is ended that I see
I am the unit every one of them together
is measurable by, if I
could ever be one of their number

& remember
you somersaulting up the scaffolding
darkening the sky above us,

how, with your help
they built the house so high
that neither you nor I can now dismantle it,
how in its shadow I am impotent & you an imp

that in the mind had birth,
that in the world if one can learn
his application, always tells its truth.

Eternal Image

The spider's legs
scrabbling on the glass
inside the jar

& the ticking of the kitchen clock

I can't show you the spider
except to say
it's bigger than I knew
spiders grew to be this way

& when I thought it'd escaped
the hair rose
over all of me
it was at least that huge

Another Bird

You found the thing
& it was hurt &
came easily into your hands.

Alone, you might'v nurtured it —
but one among a group
you gave in to its demands,

& trod the life from it. A recognition —
what fear is here
I do not want to crush,

& do. You come to tell me
what's been done
to let me know to what group you belong

while seeming to remove yourself from it.
Sanctimonious
I shout. *You* come

replete with reasons why it had to be —
you've studied grownups.
But since you killed

what you are speaking of
it doesn't matter
what you say, I say.

My morning's wounded —
I wish that all of you had been
indifferent, & left it

say to fate. Or brought the living form
stupified with hope
into our home

& all the trouble we'd'v taken on
to no end probably
but to make fear our friend,

before we buried it.

Sonnet

Fire's here, that won't be forgotten.
Nor will light, & ways to shade it.
The fire too has a stony hearth
to keep it in its place,
Chairs will not & nor will tables
fade from the mind, walls & roof make shelter
because of cold & wind.
Dispose them in what attitudes one will

if belief seduces you to show the way —
else nothing can appear
in this place that's not this house
where the intermittent ground-beat
of those flames & what they feed on
sounds like wind against an obstacle.

Because

the garage hasnt any proper floor but earth
that turns to mud, we dug a shallow ditch
across the field that slopes down from the
house, today the ducks drink from it.

Today I know one cause why men go to war.

Oh, the chores undone.

Beyond the Constellations
Here & Now

Those two lights
lower than the others
I know are houses
because the hill,
invisible, they stand on,
stands in memory,
saving me from what I see.

Another kind of call

'I love these owls that are
all invisible around us'

let that be the appeal defined

I shall not elude this life we are

Small intervals

however I elect
to understand, there will be more

I thrill

three times,
                    to hear the call

to write these words

that you also do hear .

A Nest

The first nest
discovered in a hedge
containing eggs
was wonderful

way past the edges
that day made, for now
the marvel & the vision
together come once more

I see I saw what spoke
of shapes like it I held
within my self, & how
my joy would be material

of correspondent kind,
speech surrounded me from birth,
& the weaving of what came to hand
as mouth, was I

to be the center always
or some form
more recognizable, for who
was drawn on to discover

what drew wonder
from its contents that
grew wonderful so held,
such joy's its own reward

that has within its
dynamism the demand
to tell of it, & be
what it can't understand.

"If you touch me"

If you touch me intimately
I am lost. Times fuse
in memory as limbs
of men & women loved in
various lusts. Tonight

returning from the river
home, the fog'd got there first
& though a road be known
as well as one's own flesh,
its strangeness then is
terrifying. There is, as Rilke said,
& says, a beauty in it too —

is it my self I struggle with,
stupid with limitation,
allowing me to see
too few of the signs
translatable to touch
upon the wheel I need
for life —
                    at one point we were out of it,
a half-moon showed beyond mistake
the body a fog is,
                    infiltrating all declivities
& pouring over English Hill as water
from the river in a flood.
                              But that half
my shadow has prevented me
reflecting on —
                    earlier
we looked ridiculous
with swim-suits — more,

crippled, cut in two. Words
do not say it — an old cry

that the mind pry
till with a wave of feeling words
in their distinctions can't quite match
some poem like a storm
shall bring its night to stand

— but who
shuts me out from what I know
in every sense
in this one element that's solely
the imagination's?
                    The women
had discarded them, I saw, as I
swam back,
lapped in a permission
happy in its terms,
that made it sure —

in that sun their skin, their breasts
are whole with, took on a steady glow. Here
shone their sexual hair, & here
the willows whose odor fills the air. Naturally
I looked, then looking
into my mind's seeing, looked again
as the afternoon was long. A calmness
rippled with such presence
touched my mind.

                    We men too,
undressed, spoke so
words were specific

gravities, no matter that
what each thought to talk about
was sometimes trivial. Somehow
I was more compact,
compact with the mass of detail
we grew to be among.
                              What would one
work up, to say or see,
that might'v seized the mind if they or we
stayed clothed —

I don't write *hidden,*
the skin that seals us in
has commonality enough
to show me that. & that
the one I choose
because I chose
to follow one current of this force
was absent,
& I felt the lack,

no other words will say this,
& *I love you* can be decisive
as it's uttered,
                    although the many currents run
from upstream down

& though we dressed before we left
& I shall need that time, as this, again
at some time that won't be both,
thinking to fear the loss of my singleness,
afraid there is nothing else.

to Sherril

Die Ann, Diana . . . in that night,
before the dream, I woke
beside you, went outside —
an owl hooted in the grove & looking
up, was looking up my mother's
skirts, the feathery black sway

the stars gleamed through
to be obscured . . .

I shone the flashlight on him
as she flew away.

Bildungsroman

About a month later, not having seen Hoot, we received a telephone call from Harvey Chrifield, a man who lived in a small town about 3 miles east of us. Hoot had apparently not learned his lesson about the dangers of landing on strange porch rails and peering into windows. Fortunately for him, he was greeted this time with a proffered piece of beefsteak instead of being bludgeoned with a bat. Rather than leave him with the kindly strangers, we brought him home & returned him to his cage.

One morning, almost a year later, we found Hoot's cage door open. That was the last we saw of him for 5 weeks. Then a telephone call came from Harvey Chrifield; Hoot was back with them, & for the second time we got him & returned him to his cage.

In 1959 Hoot crawled out an opening in the bottom of his cage & disappeared. 3 weeks later he turned up once more at the Chrifields'. . . . We have no idea why he flies away from our home area so rapidly, unless the wild owls are quick to drive him away when he enters their domain. In the small town, Hoot may have found safety from the wild horned owls. But the mystery of why he chose the Chrifields' house for refuge, in preference to all others in town, we probably shall never know.

(from *The World of the Great Horned Owl,* by Ronald Austing.)

The Lyre Bird

The lyre bird
amid the eucalyptus
listening for every sound he hears
to trip him into sound he makes.
He has no call or song
his own. He imitates. Each time
he utters something chances are
it is his soul that speaks.

Born again

Let me be born again. Let me
literally be spirited
back within my mother who
equally miraculously
let be live as once she was,
with me inside her belly. Let
me decide just where & when
& in what set of circumstances I
shall this time choose to enter,
let me think.

A Reason

All this month exploring — & the maps
we make when we get back
for no other reason than delight
in making maps —

but returning to the bluffs
each rock & tree, each turn
trails take beyond what then
was known to us,

become more vivid —
as the words we find to give them.

To & Fro

If I wrote to each friend I never meet these days —
to my mother in the grave —
if the landscapes of my dreams could be around me
wittingly —
if I could be naked with the woman who wants me,
the woman I desire today
& more besides those two —
or a throng of people came to talk & be with us —
if I never had to work for hire again —
if I could master the guitar —
then I could listen to the sense of revolution,
to the facts of mass & number,
to the wildflowers burning
& all this day, their first back here this year,
the redwing blackbirds' call returning.

Pond

Preface

Thus the griffin
born in the thoracic ganglion
of the desire to throttle
& determination not to

& in the lumbar constellance
because the tension gathering
demands the sinuous
relief a feline tail would be

as, above, the nape
craves wings to lift —

the beak is phallic, thus the 'gold'
it mines, means the most precious
Paradise, our body
one & knit as sexual release
discovers,
                feathered & furred for love of human
hairyness

              the creature is a lie
these signs — as all Morphic possibilities — permit,
its truth is in the yearning signified:

human being with the world at odds,
perfection as I heard of her another lie,
one makes it as one can —

out from the thorax through the arms
convulsively, the tension spreads,
split wood,
              find work, or
choking, lay
hands on our good to smother it,
                              or tell,
the words of that release up from the throat,
that tree, of truth, the tongue
talking to know ease,
known though the speech be written
blow by blow throughout the arms, as these.

The Thing Itself

A sort of mudhole. You can't see further in
than one hand's depth. I've heard friends
refusing, they'll make a joke of it
or plead that it's insanitary, or just sulk

& remembered when I've felt that way about
what can't be trusted. & shall again.
How shall I choose to recognize it now —
this evening, reading in Plotinus

that the One is overflowing, is a spring
wherefrom derives a stream
going forth, but with
no diminution
to its source. No will
nor a desire inheres —

till people dam it
called into action by its being there,
their toil a prayer
& prayers, as tears, are answered in their being born –

no matter that a reason'll be found,
to water cattle, or increase the value
of the property — what we did as boys
with sticks & mud in storms along the gutters
proves these mere afterthoughts, attenuated means
to maintain the mind by finding that the world is fixe

Divine the Spring, & Will the Dam,
Divine Will makes this Pond. Before we ever knew
it took place here, as much a presence as a language
in the world,

as a language
is a world — whose gusts
are persons in that race of winds —

rippling toward the reeds,
rippling over by the willow,
as the surface slightly lifts to break the light
with dark until it's vivid
as a mind whose choice is made.

The wavelets from the others
disturbed the metrics of my breathing
breaking the steady crawl

Not the National Geographic nor
Gargaphia, though thought could make it so,
clustering about the day like nymphs

Staring at my mind
till a shoulder or a thigh
tore apart its pictures meant to hold the scene

& I, if I was it, subsided
into being everywhere
that sense obtained .

He allowed as how he'd seen
ponds much like this one.
One was better. Which one in
particular. No, he said,
Just One.

We bound what we can never be,
but the feel of the unbounded
is this body known through me.

"I see young men, my townsmen, whose misfortune's
to have inherited limbs, bodies, heads & hands, presences; for these are more easily acquired than gotten
rid of. Better if they had been born pure spirit, &
suckled by a sylph, for then they might've seen with
clearer eyes what field they're called to labor in".

You would'v been beautiful
naked. Then who persuaded you your fat
means ugliness. Yet so it is,
you will not give or take another way,
& so it is.

The shock of fat,
like How did
that get here, is tragedy
decodable in all such increment —

our deaths are real
& births, in sum, & dieting
is quieting, to lose that ugly
bulge, ugly, like death,
because it's turned away.

The wanderer, who wouldn't swim,
wanting the mystery, to woo the women,
wanting the mystery of the expected cues,
a smack-head, so they said.

Man learned to speak & write
as I've learned recently
by studying a spider. She spins
thread from her mouth it seems,
tedding it out with her front limbs,
a web to climb by,
snare for food, a home, an early
warning system,
large extension of herself,
but don't stop there, the body
though attenuated beyond act,
abstracted from its source,
is everywhere.

Man learned to speak & write
as I've learned recently
by studying these growing things

we stop growing when we're 21
yet all around the grasses trees the vegetables
                              keep growing
in envy & desire to emulate
this human being began

o burgeon, the wildoat growing till the seed
orne on each passing wind
e sown

/e learn to speak
To have a figure for
hese moods to
ave us from them, them from us

kin, one with the evident muscle of the upper arm,
olid in its cushions of fatty tissue, & the gold hairs
listening —
          How each person, in the flesh, what? of
im, of her, or that he or she is, I know with a shock
s utterly the law of that unique conformation. The
hock of flesh we are. Who wouldnt want to speak to
his marvel. Whatever ends suggest themselves. Dress-
d, undressed, let me address you. "Lets be quiet
ow".

/ho spread the rumor, there would be enough, just
o, no more than enough. The founder of all tor-
urers. "Touch turns the nots into their own flame."
The taste of another's tongue. Human odors where
iint & willow mingle. Then the weight of the naked
eet over the mud, moving away from me. But sight is
n all of these, & all of these are words. Bend toward
ie, let me hear them — see the droplets glister, the
air sleek. . . . The water is human beauty, too.

These, the sources:

A spring — below where the colder water wells up
the fresher — never to be seen as long as it's fun
tioning.

Rains — news of the world — "The Seven Seas"
mostly in storm that cause overflow along the spi
way, — where the spearmint flourishes, so fragran
crushed underfoot, — & muddy the pond.

Fogs — distilling out of banks amorphous as a hunc
— the way a hunch comes over you till you can't s
anything else — that this is, for instance, fog, too.

Seepage — along fault-lines etc — the banks soakii
weeks since it last rained — this memory of how tl
ground is hereabouts during a storm.

    * * *

Pond rather the name of a shape, since water occu
in many forms. Thales, for example. The heron mac
it another pond that morning — since mingled in wi
each of the others.

Heat dries it up, little by little, making it possible
swim in. Whenevere it's at its fullest, it's too chill. I
September, it gets a bit foetid.

Enough of sources.

illing the lungs with air, the strong swimmer flies in
is element; the amphibian bringing the mammal to
ontentment through the reflected scene that shatters
o re-form distorted by his wake, such distortion be-
ng unavoidable for him to be there at all. The way
his is a metaphor.

inhabit a small
ortion of this world that people call
onoma County. Born in
London England, the chief
haracter of many plays & novels,
en of late on film,"
ot visited by me since 1958,
may never touch on it again.

ow huge this planet
e inhabit, yet the mind
an make it everywhere, it seems

nly the locus it inhabits
gs behind, but soon
ne sheds that handicap.

eavy breasts
o bra contains
hin blouse
f a word that *heavy* is
ie nipples darkly stain.

"How fortunate to've been handed a slave to accompany one throughout this life! For so experience
among my fellows convinces me this body is. No
wonder one resents so unwearying a helpmeet, & tries
to poison him continuously. Yet will one raised to be
a slave make a good master? Nor will one easily elect
to be judged by the appearance of his servant".

"Life is passing me by".

If you are dragged
as intimated in your voice
talking about life
& how you think it
should be organized

how shall I listen, life
is not for you the feeling
rising from the organs
that they are for me.

TUI

⚊ ⚊

Lake, mist, the Joyous — a final
condition on the yin side, & belonging
therefore to Autumn.

Fog steadily encroaching throughout these last 10 days —
mid-July now: California.

Some sun to warm the top 2 feet
beneath which, a deep chill — & swimming
we mix the zones.

The sign will be on you
is the abstraction from
multiple transactions one
woman is this instance of.

We met her at the pond,
she told of the commune on a nearby farm, her residence
where they raise rabbits — Oh, my wife says,
who had a rabbit for a pet, For pets?
Oh no, we eat them
the damsel made reply,
& as she rose to dress
almost we saw her cottontail
but the ears hung from her chest.

The swallows skim the surface . . .
after bugs, or drink, or a glimpse of
their reflections.

We discuss the possibilities
though what will change the sight of them
that holds us talking here.

You can't say words are not enough
& expect to be believed
nor not to be.

In early infancy I knew
to read intent in every mind about me.
And this so terrified
I chose to lose the power
& fell to speech, & lost all memory
of infancy, but what speech gives to me.

What does this message
intend on my body. This
is the acid test
I'd here engrave.

Those benignly felt hallucinations
throughout '66 — the Golden Horde,
one called the men on ponies headed
through golden prairies westward —
post-coital, that prior to then,
sexual release had never loosed —

information more basic then than reproduction.
Now I was allowed to let it slip, as *done*
where *I* is cultural too:

North American coastal consciousness, in the 4th
(was it?) year of USA's massive intervention in
masses of Consequent Reasoning).

The mounting excitement
as we move
step by step
of difference
off the same

f wants to be the same

The same as *is*

he astonishing brilliance
of the first time

Of Death Yes
It can be said

We fall in love with what we can't
see through. If we can't discover
how it's done — this is called
enchantment. Seeing how it works
is to see the trick it is — as Oz

— as *we* is more fitting somehow
than the *I*, of course it's one alone who writes
except the words are talking

— the lungs inflate with air
The arms & hands move laterally
The legs kick down

into the murk will
work for anyone.

"It is an interesting question how far men & women
would retain their relative rank if they were divested
of their clothes".

Should I footnote that.

"They were as misled, to allow their desire for the
bizarre & uncommon to take over, as my contem-
poraries are, to think the common & the everyday
not strange".

"The one mystery left is form, & the morphology
of same" — Aphrodite
her path up from the pond
& hers.

Ken   ———————   mountain, keeping still

      ——   ——   meditation which, by
                          keeping external things
                          quiescent, lights up the
                          inner world

K'an   ——   ——   water, the abysmal . . .
      ———————   represents Eros & considered
      ——   ——   the opposite of Logos . . .
                          kidneys . . . sexuality . . . the Moon

This is the truth of the pond atop this hill —
Heaven entered water through the one —
the only Fall's the Fall

. . . Men would expose themselves to her nearly every
day on the NYC subway. It got to be so she would
look first at a man's crotch & not merely fearfully.

Mystification clothes the Mystery.
what words'll bring one to their edge.
The mudhole of my body.

A Diction

Keep all my actions cool O Muse,
don't let me use a word
I wouldn't use.

"Few of the passengers even glance at the sights on
the route, for they are predominantly Romans on
humdrum errands. Every day they pass – & ignore –
romantic ruins, historic & religious shrines, & archi-
tectural gems that thrill tourists by the millions"

"If our experience is destroyed, our behavior will be
destructive"

"Bion relates the origin of thought to the experience
of no-breast"

"Whenever they need a tall blonde" she comments "I
stand a chance. . . . What producer has enough imagination or courage to cast a film in which the wife is
much taller than her husband? . . . I was impressed
with him . . . because he was taller than I – there's
that height thing again . . ." Vital measurements:
39-26-38 . . . who, after 10 years in show biz, "still
can't get anyone to consider me as anything but a sex
object".

One sees for miles
& 20-20 vision in this light discloses
detail — leaves on those eucalyptus trees
for instance —

the skin of loins & legs can't see
the substance that supports & presses
& caresses it —

as above,
so below.

Why not, since we do at the pond, go naked in our
homes. His tone was reasonable — i.e., slightly queru-
lous. The silent halls of Context.

One couple we know were hosts to another, who during several weeks persistently came naked to the
breakfast table, though it would have been as easy to
dress before as after that meal. Did they pretend to
themselves that their behavior did not in fact consti-
tute a message? As it might do, to close the door
when you're undressing or getting dressed.

We know what mutual nakedness has meant. We may
not be sure what we want it to mean, except that it
be something other than before. There was a word,
reason: it would find a life with us, naked in our
contexts.

From a little distance, it's a wise father knows his
own son, among the throng by the pond.

Bios/Bias: to-be-alive. As Rimbaud said, We are all slopes.

"The people who had got off the trucks had to undress. I well remember a girl, slim & with black hair, who, as she passed close to me, pointed to herself & said: Twenty-three years old."

One thinks of nakedness as something one is bound to attend to. And so one does, there, but not constantly: the human being will not be stared at. Besides, the entire hill, with its sky, wants one's attention too. And nakedness, attended *from,* is a healing ritual. The sky is naked too. Thus it encloses also the hawks we watch, & it is no longer necessary to shoot them in order to bring motion from an alien world into one's own.

"When we speak of mind we mean, above everything else, consciousness. It means, before everything else, memory. Memory may lack amplitude; it may embrace only a feeble part of the past; it may retain only what is just happening; but memory is there, or there is no consciousness. A consciousness unable to conserve its past, forgetting itself unceasingly, would be one perishing & having to be re-born at each monent: & what is this but unconsciousness? But all consciousness is also anticipation of the future. To retain what no longer is, to anticipate what as yet is not, — these are its primary functions. Consciousness is the hyphen."

"For while they thought they were unseen in their secret sins, they were sundered one from another by a dark curtain of forgetfulness, stricken with terrible awe, & sore troubled by spectral forms."

"Oh Children! *The hour has struck by the clock Dont mean shit to him*"

"She is the only one who places her hands over the priest's on the chalice, not self-conscious about physical contact, wholly intent on the sacrament"

"With these things it is just as it is when one enters water. One can tell for oneself whether it's warm or it's cold. Likewise a person must convince oneself of these experiences, then only are they real".

"They have been seen occasionally, on the damp freshly-manured ground in a nursery garden wheneve one stamped on the soil, & in muddy ditches or i ponds when one stirred the waters in them.

The resemble tiny flames, about 1/2 inch to 5 inches hig & not more than 2 inches broad. Sometimes they ar right on the ground, at other times they float about inches above it. That they dance about is apparentl not true. What really happens is that they go ou suddenly while another flame arises quite near, & th probably accounts for the impression of rapid mov ment. Occasionally they are blown along by the win a few feet before they become extinguished.

In many cases when one puts one's hand in the litt flame, no heat is to be felt; dry reeds do not cat fire.

Generally there is no smell, occasionally a faint sme of sulphur.

What do these mysterious flames consist of? Nobod has yet succeeded in collecting the gas that takes fir Such gases can arise by the decomposition of rotti substances.

Dancing like tiny flames over the churchyard, or e ticing travelers into the morass."

"No, it is not an optical illusion, nor a contrast phenomenon.

(i) survey the whole lawn, & note how the light increases near your shadow.
(ii) take a few steps: you will see the glow of light go with you, & places where the light was not particularly bright become illuminated as your shadow approaches.
(iii) compare your shadow with that of other people; you will see the Heiligenschein surrounding only your own head. This may lead you to philosophize!

When Benvenuto Cellini noticed it, he thought the shimmer of light was a sign of his own genius!"

Summertime

—in the morning, often, working in the garden, a time belonging to the esophagus/ stomach/ anus constellance, content is utter — passes as sleep about a dream, the dream, my recent sleep.

As the heat increases, as the hours mount since last I had nicotine, as the childhood habituation of *school* once again makes itself felt in the too-early drawing-up of awareness into the thorax/ tongue/ nape constellance, — I start to hanker for the pond.

On my way there, the landscape I traverse has my attention: yet isn't this the attention creating that landscape that announces, with each minute, my distance from, & closeness to, the pond.

coincidentally, memories of swimming will suffuse me — yet this is not the same as to swim in actuality. Thus one continues.

Much like a sentence I proceed. I term this duration. Thus measure, metric, stem from the periodicity these various processes instruct one in.

One attends from various modes of awareness. So-called genital organization means that the star of nerves at the spine's base becomes focus of the mind. Different people know different rhythms of moving from one such focus, to the next.

There is an imagination of the world which is utterly debauched. It proscribes the time & place for certain activities, arguing that such procedure is the most efficient. But it never asks what the origin is, of its definition of efficiency.

The
White-Tailed
Kite

The penis
straining
with the same
attention

Such is its vantage,
how can it help but
discover
what it needs

Never saw it catch
a single thing in
this field — yet

time & again it
returns, by its torn
wing identifiable —

the worry over readers —
must be
one place where it feeds

The both of us

so *in*
in this
perusal
of potential

Filled with
this possibility
of the instant
next to this

Wings raising must
contain implicitly
the movement
consequent

Nailed to the invisible
it cannot
flutter just to
flutter

Time & again I
watched, as though you
came to tell me something,

as though your patience
were a lesson —
but how to think

you patient, or
its opposite, the wings
blur as you focus

One never shall
discover him self
here & now

unless an
elsewhere have
declared its

whereabouts
demanding one
attend, & here

takes care
now of itself,
attended from

I will, I won't —
a kind of nothingness
I guess, although I know

it's air, seeing
how it buffets you
by your adjustments

in the face or
force of it,
supports you there &

thus you hover
& will have to
plunge through

& into it,
to verify
your hope

If the field were
more abundant, or
your kind less so,

still you'd have to hover —
that's what you are,
a harrier,

whatever the conditions that
permit your presence,
this side death

Now gone, yet
what you pointed to

in me
stirs in this

field, as an attention
focusses, & thus is

focussed,
here

At last!
these visits &
these visitations come
to roost — your white

flash, if edged with
black — & all
falls into place
at the edge of that

intrusion —
again — the welcome
could be death's —
you've got to be

my habit — nothing
holds you up —
it's on such you flutter,
on & off — no, on

Maybe you're exhausted,
in an agony of hunger
hanging there, pinioned to
yourself, & the invisible

Your life — I
cannot save —

registers
a wonder, here —

or I hang
agonized & dumb,
agonized, I mean,
if dumb

Make it of metal —
it doesn't eat what it
soars over, but
disintegrates

what can't be borne
again

Wanting the activity in words —
as you want yours — how else
could the young of either

kind, begin to live —

I mean delight, a simple
(complicated) launching into

motion — it leads
on, to something else,
to eat, as it was meant

Kite meant
greed, you eat,
or previous
of your kind, were
thought to eat,

too avariciously —
men's judgment,
the creature that is capable
of falling back, going
slack, inventing the absurd

The Night of the White-Tail Kite

Fred Astaire had bony wrists, the veins
over the big hands
stood up, as in the vision of my mother's
father — as mine do

The dance-step he had shown me
is no use unless he sponsor me
but waking in the grand hotel
I read the headlines: Fred Astaire
Stricken in NYC

In a kind of intermission, I dragged all through
some department-store, looking for a pair of pants
no-one else would wear

The musical Chuck Brown dug & promised
me the Panthers'd promote on Broadway
can't get off the ground now Chuck Brown's
disappeared — gone underground or maybe
been assassinated

Long distance to Chicago —
long distance to LA —
the phone-lines tapped —
his widow, if she is,
sends my *ms* back, the pictures of her husband
have newsprint taped across them —

I must drag through each apartment
in every ghetto looking
before I can produce
the art-work for these times

Waking actually, to find my wife
also dreamt a department-store to spend her
waking sleeptime in

Guilty with the weight felt
of the myriad dream details
this omits

I think of you, my form
that gives the name to this
so one is warned

My looking is
not "idle
curiosity,"
"idling my
time away"

but an avidity
— even as
avidity's a
favorite word —

I devour it
even as it lives on

Its favorite meadow lies
on that aspect from this house
I feel the most
open to
invasion

Where the sun
rises, thus
drives night

back through the house
& over English
Hill — leaving

through the eucalyptus
stand that never
sheds it utterly

Those trees that crowd together
making single shadows so
much more, a thing
so singularly lessening

There grows a mystery
on their far side, half
within that shade,

for all we eat its
fruit we might'v bought with less
expenditure of sweat

A Period

The spade
unearths them
every time, think how

the whole
county underneath its
skin must swarm with them,

how interpreting that
dream'll demonstrate
— just thought that Freud

Astarte or A
Step or Gaze lived close
across the gully from her

childhood home — how
curved the cord connecting
here to everywhere,

now, dense, this
medium has proved
most fruitful, then say,
to Olduvai.

The imagination
seizes on
some further
series of itself

which, to be
most fully, it'll
try to let
fill with itself —

the first itself is,
the next *itself* is
that entity that hovers
within range of one's

senses, causing distance
instantly to radiate
as the touch of one
one loves —

the imagination being
this phrase one learns
to fit to one's
imagination, listening

to others in
their use,
abuse, of it, the throat
aching, thus the tongue

flutters & the lips
distinguishing
say wings, say
things, the risk

the only way to fly,
whitened with yourself,
or your determination
to be absent from that site,

as all before you sings
— yet is the first itself
a creature of your will alone,
a bird has led mine home

In the bisected brain
a book I read this winter
I read of how the head
can be split open carefully

so that the right
side doesn't fathom
what the left side finds,
unless one side can focus

on some facet of the world
in such a way the other
reads cues from the body's
posture given in

such focussing —
I felt the truth of this
without conducting such experiments
but the passage

set so in another discourse
held me with the hope
its author'd be brought to
recognize its grounds

The thing about attention
is Bergson said of consciousness
is waiting for the instant
always coming from the long gone

into birth — there are other modes of being
meditation knows
but poetry knows
itself in time disclosed

If all I've been among
has shaped my mind
sometimes it's machinery
that races, gears

unable to engage —
or mind made such machines
first knowing them —
but you are something else

I couldn't make,
we come from the same
craftsman, as people used to think,
who want to find a cause

How else should words
that come to me create
you here, begun
before I understood

what I had recognized,
how alien you are,
familiar
as my mind

The FM undercurrent
as I'm in this place
alone without the strength
to joy in solitude

today, just then
attending to an ad,
taken with the tone,
how he isn't able,

if he wants to sell,
to sound as though he
takes it seriously —
all such intentions these days

verge on this in language,
either we
have to laugh or
the propagandist does —

but once I found a letter
like from Whitman's God
dropped on the street
& spent an evening

figuring it out —
not to mention diaries
read illicitly, for instance
Leslie P's

Did that wing mend
or are you "your"
own child —

the fledgling of last summer
grown — a fence
has grown between this house

& the meadow I call yours —
two further houses built
along this slope last winter —

as a child, a word conveying
ice & snow — snow
fell one day up here

this winter, most unusually —
but wet it was,
& wet & wind inform it,

& wing's a rime,
a question i.e. about time,
that's always here, as *I am*

This beating is
about the pace
my eyes

when hunger occupies
me oscillate
& speech

Almost March again
with intermittent
rain —

the lady Emerson
became
is virgin strobe

Today you chased
crows from your
cypress tip

I guess it's
nesting time
but how to say *again*

Looks like we can't
stay in this place
another year,
next spring

thought thinks,
my wife & I
won't get to watch you
so, as if we'd

died, perhaps we shall have,
& so much left to
think, & such sights
left to — you

are so
neat, no excess anything
— flew right by the house

My soul
tells me the tale
that spirit has to hear —

that I
shall be a bird
precisely as it's spoken

how you are,
but not as *ghost*
says it or *haunts*,

in a different
instance the same
difficulty, how to say *again*

Father wrote me
Mother loved the birds —
I can't conjure her,

had forgotten that
& many other facts
her presence bore —

she refuses
even to appear
in dreams —

what force
I can not harness
hastens her away

who was my world
& listener —
so I'm enabled

to hover & invoke
these other images,

to make a tale

that says she is
this bird, that shows
its shadow

wavering
where grasses
shake the wind

It is revealed
through the agency of miracle
this poem has you there

so that no other
Presence
may descend from Heaven —

yet he ascended so
enabled by the Crucifixion
that I may read as disbelief —

or doubt, the horizontal
that means all that our earth
holds possible, & ties our hands

to contravene the Heavenward —
yet language speaks of the
miraculous, & forms

Now more of a meadow, less of a skyward identity. I
saw Jesus walking in the meadows of Heaven, sometimes it was Paradise. Little children — such as then I
saw, though I did not need to place myself among
them — gathered where He went. Thinking back,
there were a few trees, tall grasses, he wore those
flowing cloudy robes. . . . It will not come clear. It
did not need to come clear. I was there. I did not
need to place myself there. If I had thought what
name to give my feeling at this scene, it might have
been Exuberance, Tranquility, Assurance. In the
movie to be made of Tolkein's Hobbit, — but it is our
Hobbit now, — how will hobbits appear? I know very
well what one is, although I can't for the life of me
describe one in detail. Or, in detail, sure, but *one*? As
the voice speaking of Jesus fell away, as those flakes
of stone from about the form emerging.

Where Christ's significance is thought to be the plot-
ting of the individual life at crisis amid informing
actuality, unquote, a small shadow hovers on & above
the vision, hungry for definite shape.

Why speak of I he dreams

You don't catch much
in this place,
are you a habit

that the mind would break,

looking for a greater
measure of exactitude
than the field will bear

Point, to indicate
this place before my
self, I would be moving

to occupy at once,
that *at once* live
as for the first time –

& again, & everywhere
thrusting forth
at once.

So the heart'll
flutter just
prior to agony
I'll never need to name —

the animal
your talons
pierce to seize —

The motion of I am
The animal all
terror I have been
together for the first time

yet again

You — is a presence
that the world has
in one's feeling as
though another person

kept one company —
aware
that birds can't fathom
human speech

nor its notation,
one might seem mad
so to address a being
knowing it can't hear —

yet from infancy this process
is a means wherewith
to glimpse those othernesses
& as if

mere intermitted light cast
shadows on a two-dimensioned
space, within one's face
shapes shift,

& if imperfectly,
still in the skull
the earth'll be
atonement soon enough

The left brain to the right —
or if left-handed, right to left —
ahoy, what's going on out there,

give me some word —
& auricle to ventricle
enforce the beat

Singular, attentive, wrapt,
alone, aloft, a flutter,
so much causality
slips through the grasses
whose tips disperse such seeds

You'd been one with
& became the sign of
the magic of that place.

Yesterday we left for ever,
as if our hearts could break. Today
near our new place

one just like you came
to obliterate such specialness
& keep the faith.

Bloomfield, July 1970 - March 1972

Proofs

The way the land falls away is the first fact. Breath-taking. Said I guess because such a view impels an imagination of how it would be, to plunge down into it, so you'd get too much air & that'd take your breath away? It's a feeling from a dream I'm calling on. We find we're falling, then recall how to unfold our wings, so we soar.

Indeed the soul has its flights. In Siberia the shamans flew many hundreds of miles. As one would have to, to get any place, the distances are so great, there. Can we take such accounts as literal. We want to see a photo, better, a movie. Better yet, be present, best, be ourselves the seer. What a wish! Best forgotten, along with all the machinery of magic carpets, which already begins to forget the truth of these events, — & the machinery of B 52s, which completes the erasure.

It's the "viewless wings of poesy" that are meant, but that language grows thin & bent with age — true as it is. For language can take us there — wherever it is. Keats is present, & the difficulty we have with him is precise testimony, that this is John Keats, 1795-1821. who confronts us, & not another. The old are hard to understand, how they appear to speak of a different world & have small tolerance for ours. They take some listening to. Keats, at 178, is very old. But still alive. We can't see him however. And in this place, it's difficult to deny the primacy of sight, literally what light & the eyes bring in, for we're 600 feet up on a hillside in open country & that furthest line of mountains is 70 miles off. You look into it & go into a trance. You are everywhere within view. A powerful sensation. Helpless, also, for there's nothing you can do about that brush-fire down towards your fingertips. Your intelligence can't travel with the light rebounding from your brain. Powerful lonely.

But we share this other reading of the words to do with light & sight: Ah now I see, Came the dawn, my cherished insights, I'm in the dark. These phrases accompany a return of intelligence, we speak them *to* someone, a present person or the custom of relation that makes a kind of presence, as if another were here.

So much gets said. . . . I think of the unending winter rains, the storms driving laterally until eventually some of the stuff starts to seep through the cracks in the timber, all is a howl, the gutters of the roof muttering along, the windows bend inwards with the force as though someone leaned on our eyes — & today the grass is white with summer drought. The only water available has been caught in tanks & ponds. Talking will not make a poem, even though the one impulse informs both.

When I consider form in language, of language, what withstands & what doesn't, I think of that other mystery, that any created life contains as it reveals. A poem is very like a person. We can describe him, mimic him even, & as we live with him, begin to know when he is false, when true, to who he is. Learning his history, we can see how he got to be that way. But he got to be that way without the (dis)advantage of such hindsight. The track of the serial solutions he's present evidence of, return us to his conception. But no matter his father & mother meant what they did, it was not him they could have meant. And when someone gives him- or her-self to the language for love of the poetic impulse, the offspring will be no carbon of the poet's intention. Consider too the question of the usefulness of poetry. We need to confront, as though it were the same question, the other, What is the usefulness of a human being?

People delight us, incense us, or leave us cold: according to our response, we may or may not make use of them, but this concern is secondary. Who'll persuade us to attend to the causes of our various responses, if not ourselves?

Today, with the proofs before me of a book I quit writing a year & a half since, it all came back to me — not actually, for the marvel of that place I speak of tonight as "this place," inheres in its being precisely where it is, 8 miles southwest of the house I sit in; but in the remembrance I mean, which can be a suffocating mode of attention until imagination uses its tissues to breathe new life with. Which makes clear my present impulse. The proofs prove I was there, & wrote. But imagining I was reading them as another, I began to see a further poem, whose parts are the poems of these proofs.

Being open rangeland, heavily populated with jack-rabbits & smaller rodents, this place supports birds of prey in profusion, as well as the largest of all, the turkey-vultures who clean up the livestock carcasses etcetera. I'd never lived where so many were to be found & my fascination led me to an ornithologists' guide, *Birds of the West*. With difficulty, — for an encyclopedia precedes the particularities it would account for, — I identified these creatures, the red-tail hawks, the sparrow-hawks, the white-tail kites, the barn owls, the great horned owls. All are birds of prey & all have keen sight, & seeing how I was entranced with them, I stood against the trance by making forms with it in this other, relational seeing, & in this a-literal form of flight grounded myself against the wish their soaring & hovering roused in me. — Seeing how often *trance* is a word that comes into this account, I consulted the dictionary to find it has a root in *transir,* to perish; which catches something of my intent with it, that life need to come to see what it's about. What is only specific in us — the animal which imagined being human — can in turn come to rescue us from the stupor of human history, that inertial system whose vividnesses are humanity's seeing through the merely animal daze. Living a language one is in a like fix, & inhabiting a poetry & a literature, also will know this double take. I took my forms among the shapes in language my excitement in the presence of these birds started from their burrows — I mean wherever in the person the roots of speech may be. There was no prior conclusion as to what these forms would be, & that's by now a convention in itself, though by its very nature it looks to be the last word on the subject. We'll see.

I took attention, in various of its modes, as the matter, that is I found these modes subjected me to the mystery of their existence. What else should I do. Living, one is emplaced, & such was the spirit of that place, & to breath at all's to be inspired. A tranced looking, an unremitting attending; these went on where I stood, & where the creature causing me so to stand, hovered. The white-tail kite is such an angelic fact of the second mode that in attending with it, attention itself was all my attention.

Psychologists of a certain persuasion have given us the terms *attending to* & *attending from.* The example clearest to my mind I take from Michael Polanyi's *The Tacit Dimension.* "In the case of a human physiognomy, I would now say that we rely on our awareness of its features for attending to the characteristic appearance of a face. We are attending *from* the features *to* the face, and thus may be unable to specify the features." I take the so-called unconscious to be, at any moment, what we attend from. Now, as a poet, I've taken to heart Robert Duncan's definition of the poetic act as an adventure in consciousness: though I can nowhere find the passage in his works tonight, so I'd best assume it as I can, as my own directive. In writing, I've wanted to leave no stone unturned, to incorporate into the poem all its grounds. Taken to its limit in me this has proved Sisyphean & there are, in *Threads* & *The Ends of the Earth,* poems to prove that assertion. I mistook the risk the selection of the incidents must be, & lost trust in the power of language. Words can't be multiplied to be the actual without too great a sacrifice of that clarity words can give. My hunch is that I spoke of a world in common while speaking to & of that white-tail kite. Is this bird a symbol then. I offer instead of that argument this discretion, if that bird is actual so is the world & all in it, & in the sequence that's named for the bird, if words work there the way sequences of meaning do in our lives, all may know a co-temporaneous existence.

The kite, one says, is innocent. But the man who makes a form with it? Is aware of the disasters our employment of unremitting attention, our mistaking of eternal vigilance, — we have the colloquial "hawks" as evidence — cause in our world. A directive inculcated in me, taking advantage of native, even specific, attributes, has often made me into a thing that has to pin it all down, fix & freeze, miserably, life's fluidities. It's at work now, & what clarity it permits I'd turn toward a release from its depravities. The kite looks to eat but a habit of attention can't even see itself. Not to present anyone, myself least of all, as some attitude of evil, as deadly, that, as the other sanctimony; but to say, no attention but may be equivocal, & I was engaged in forming what I could concerning modes of paying it.

So there's a function of the person, the "I", that's high — above it all, wide — of the mark, & handsome — to itself, self-entranced. Something hawkish here & hence my unease over the angelic nature of that particular kite — although there may have actually been two; & the incidents I'll now tell of bring in one, maybe two, more, so, ridiculously enough, I have to consider myself as guarded or haunted not by a single bird, but a cabal of them. The day after we moved to our present home, I was very depressed, at having had to move, & at dawn went for a walk in the orchard abutting the new place. I looked up & there was the, a, kite — as if to say, home is where the heart is. And today, not having seen one hereabouts for three or four months, I looked up from the beginnings of this writing to see one, close over the house. I want to insist I deplore the meaning of such so-called synchronicities — but the world insists in my despite, & it is there, not here, that any sense of life I may communicate must find its life. So "follow your star" still makes sense, & apparently the multiplication of known stars makes very little difference. I see too that the egotism of such belief transforms in poetry where the experience is to be returned to the world which bred it. But when I was writing this sequence the supposition that I should be so singled out was intolerable. So this movement of the poem I couldn't resolve. It breaks off in an enactment of my bewilderment at it.

* * *

The sequence called "Pond" here springs from the experience of the pond further up the hill from where we lived, a place where some springs had been dammed years since to water cattle during the summer drought; its present owner regards it as real estate, &

cattle no longer use it, so it makes a fine swimming-hole, & is used as such by various locals & their visitors, the one common bond being a desire to go naked in the open. Some, no doubt, put up with the rest, simply to get cool when it's over 100 in the shade. But for myself, & I'm not alone, to be naked to wind, sun & water, amid such a nature, is ecstasy.

It's lovely too, to be able to attend both to & from others equally naked, there's an ease of congress not often present in dressed dealings. And isn't the impulse to know such, akin to that impulse to reveal how we are, that informs poetry? I must think so, & have no sense this sequence arose from any necessity to distance the experience. Rather, it has to do with an illusion of timelessness felt there. Any day of the summer, the same sun, the same grasses, the one sky all blue over the one pond, the discrete bodies also entering a oneness — yet any day is itself, discrete as the person entering, for the first time, that water (a little muddier today than last week, therefore a little lower.).

From *rheein,* to flow, to rhythm, to keep time, poetry's time's stuff & accounting. But any more usual sense of rhythm-in-poetry would have defeated the pulse of the society of the pond, an intermitted, trite or prosaic series began to be the form . . . "Trite" in rhyming I mean where rhymes rhyme predictably as trunks grow on limbs, no mean relaxation of suspicion in people whose grandparents hung cloths over the legs of their furniture. The prosaic quality I see is rather the absence of that impassioned language whose root is surely an hysteria in the presence of beauty felt as lure & threat. The true beauty of ourselves & the nature we live with is the marvel of matter-of-factness.

As the pond is open to all comers, a place where
strangers naked are no stranger than friends, & all
may enjoy this uncustomary freedom in one
another's presence, one's being — I want to say *physi
cal* being, but how refuse the truth that in this inhere
the signs of all the person is? — one's being tacitly
given place with easy immediacy, no names or oc
cupations asked or given; so into this sequence came
passages from my reading, without attribution: any
who recognize the source will certainly know where
to go. I altered these passages at times, as surely the
notions I conceived of my companions there changed
them from who they remained to themselves, as clear
ly the place itself modifies the individuals who dis
pose themselves according to its shapes.

It begins to sound crowded. . . . But there are never
more than six or seven there, & many days I find
have it all to myself. Drifting with an air mattress in
the air currents, a meditative trance may take m
over, a feeling of world & self becoming one. . .
What word or phrase won't do, to fill one's mind
then, the "littlest" equal with the "largest". "Lit
tlest" alone can measure everything, one thinks
Someone complained — or maybe meant a compli
ment — of Chinese wisdom-texts, that they were so
inarticulate, their power of suggestion was unlimited
The one thing attended to lets all be attended from
Thus trapped, all, as attention reverses, is apparently
present — to such thought. It happens. And there are
quotations here from *The Secret of the Golden
Flower* to be form of such times.

At these times, so much mental activity, the making
of poems too, may come to seem trivial altogether
oddly remote attempts to realize worth in a life. The
activity may well appear a will o' the wisp — & even

now I must admit the truth that, one's intentions notwithstanding, there's no assurance that good and not ill will come to one's interference in the human world. The choice is, not to let that consideration interfere with such participation; but the mood which knows the will o' the wisp truth is real, & recurs, & has its place in this poem. But the delight in the language with which Minnaert, in his *Light & Colour,* speaks of that phantasm, revives in me tonight as I remember how I came to transcribe it.

There is a doubt, though irresoluble, at what the lyric mode in poetry, with its trammelled location of an author-itative I, comes to in our day. This isn't easy to say without sounding as though I were trying to win all ways. Clearly, I believe something is possible of it, for such is published here. But here, at the edge of a vast migration, or isn't it rather the shore the edge remorselessly has pushed beyond; seeing the land fill up, & in the bafflement of our western humanity, the wonder at what we have come to darkens despite the other awareness, that in health one loves life for the living. Each can find a location, it happens — & a language to tell it with. But the landscape falls away before us, & the literal fall of this hill may draw some of its beauty from the other terror that will not so naturally find a form. Or do I avail myself of the general & abstract to save myself from the immediate locale. I could never see it was mine to decide, for another, once I'd formed what the difficulty was — I could never see it was mine to decide for another.

Sebastopol
August 12, 1973

FORMS

Printed at The Coach House Press, Toronto
in a limited edition of 1000 copies,
October 1973.